Like Stone Soup

The Role of the Professional Development School in the Renewal of Urban Schools

By Peter C. Murrell, Jr.

AACTE

The American Association of Colleges for Teacher Education is a national, voluntary association of colleges and universities with undergraduate or graduate programs to prepare professional educators. The Association supports programs in data gathering, equity, leadership development, networking policy analysis, professional issues, and scholarship.

The opinions, conclusions, and recommendations expressed in this monograph do not necessarily reflect the views or opinions of the American Association of Colleges for Teacher Education. The AACTE does not endorse or warrant this information. The AACTE is publishing this document to stimulate discussion, study, and experimentation among educators. The reader must evaluate this information in light of the unique circumstances of any particular situation and must determine independently the applicability of this information thereto.

Like Stone Soup: The Role of the Professional Development School in the Renewal of Urban Schools may be ordered from:

AACTE Publications
1307 New York Avenue, NW, Suite 300
Washington, DC 20005-4701
Tel: 202/293-2450
Fax: 202/457-8095

Web site: http://www.aacte.org
Single copy: $19.95 AACTE members
            $24.95 nonmembers

Printed in the United States of America
ISBN No: 0-89333-167-8

CONTENTS

PREFACE

The AACTE Committee on Multicultural Education is pleased to sponsor this very important publication on the role of professional development schools in the revitalization of urban schools. The much heralded and highly publicized concept of PDSs has been touted as a model, not only for the preparation of teachers, but as a mechanism for the reform of urban schools. The proponents of professional development schools have stated that these sites would produce better trained teachers who would meet national standards of accountability and, of most urgent concern, raise the achievement levels of students.

Peter Murrell's work, however, informs us that these hoped-for goals have not been realized. He boldly and brilliantly writes that the concept of PDSs has limited application in urban schools because it has failed to unmask teachers' assumptions, prejudices, and worldviews about children of color and the communities in which they live. In addition, Murrell believes that the disconnections and the discontinuities among theory, practices, policies, partnerships, and communities are the principle reasons that PDSs have not produced significant changes in urban K-12 schools or SCDEs. Murrell concludes that professional development schools in urban sites are not the "leading edge" of reform but are mere "shrouds" that hide maintenance of an unequal and undemocratic social order.

The AACTE Committee on Multicultural Education intends this monograph as an impetus for an enriched and continuing debate on the role of professional development schools in urban districts. Most significantly, we believe that Murrell's research pushes a new vision and agenda for teacher education—collaborative partnerships as community building. His challenge to us must not be taken lightly or dismissed summarily. The future of teacher education and millions of students in urban schools depend on our commitment and resolve to face these issues.

Jacqueline Jordan Irvine, Chair
AACTE Committee on Multicultural Education

FOREWORD

This monograph is a disturbing and provocative critique of professional development schools and their role in the renewal of urban schools. I use the words "disturbing" and "provocative" carefully, and in their most positive sense. Murrell's monograph is well thought through, extremely well conceptualized and articulated; and at the same time, it will be seen as very challenging by many who advocate for, and are involved in, the PDS movement.

Murrell brings a unique perspective to the important work on PDSs and urban school renewal. As he describes it, his frame of reference is shaped by two important kinds of "dual consciousness." First, is the one identified by DuBois—the duality inherent in being a person of color in America. The second is shaped by the tensions between his academic and scholarly training and his urban and community organizing experiences. His doctoral work in human learning and cognition at the University of Wisconsin gave him the scholarly grounding and perspectives of a psychologist. Meanwhile, in graduate school, he worked as a teacher in an urban high school and an activist in community organizing around African-centered schools, and all-Black school districts. His current roles as an associate professor in the departments of psychology and education and as director of the Master of Arts in Teaching program at Northeastern University's Center for Innovation in Education provide him a way to marry these different perspectives. The focus he brings to teacher education and school reform is shaped by an understanding of how schools and teachers can help kids learn and develop, and by a keen eye on how recipients of school reform experience it.

These perspectives shape his review and analysis of the role of PDSs in the renewal of urban schools. In "Like Stone Soup," he argues that the goals of equity—reducing the performance gap between poor children of color and whites—are not well served in PDSs. In fact, he argues that PDSs can actually inhibit the development of equity by making people think progress is being made even though the issues of power, privilege, and community building are not being addressed.

As one who has been involved in one way or another with PDSs since 1989, I have watched a grass roots, marginalized movement grow to become a dominant idea in current thinking about the simultaneous renewal of teacher education and schools. Five or six years ago, Ann Lieberman and I co-presented the only PDS-related session at the AACTE Annual Meeting. At the Annual Meeting this year, there were multiple sessions on PDSs offered in each time block. As PDSs become more mainstream, and move in from the fringes in school districts and colleges, they will quite appropriately be more closely scrutinized. As PDSs become increasingly considered pathways into the teaching profession; as they become increasingly important vehicles of school reform; and as they move toward institutionalization in their schools and collegiate communities, people inside and outside of PDSs must stop and ask what is being institutionalized. Are PDSs meeting their goals?

Peter Murrell says no. One of the goals of professional development schools is the improvement of student learning. Implicit in some PDSs, and explicit in many, has been the goal of equity. Murrell argues (following the extensive literature review on PDSs and equity done by Valli, Cooper, and Frankes, 1997) that PDSs have not met this goal. Valli and her colleagues commend the Holmes Group (as the archetype PDS advocate organization) for trying to connect school reform movements like PDSs with equity and social justice; nonetheless they conclude by noting that their research shows that" most PDS partners have either not attempted or are floundering in this undertaking" (p. 299).

Murrell takes this critical look at PDSs and equity even further, arguing that PDSs not only have failed to live up to their rhetoric about equity, they actually can, as currently constructed, stand in the way of successful urban school reform. Two of the many examples from the monograph illustrate this point: In Murrell's view, the bilateral nature of most PDSs (as partnerships between schools and institutions of higher education) blocks and excludes other parties that must be involved for equity concerns to be properly addressed: parents, community members, youth and community-based organizations. Furthermore, he notes that the focus on the professional development of teachers detracts from the needs for development of parents, schools, neighborhood, and children. Murrell worries that as PDSs become more established and better defined, clearer models and approaches will be available to draw upon, and adherence to those models will take precedence over the equity challenges and the needs for improvement of urban schools.

Throughout the monograph Murrell returns to the idea of vision—
what a PDS is supposed to do. As one of the two dozen educators and
activists who helped craft the NCREST vision statement that Murrell
cites, I can recall that the understanding and commitment to equity
varied considerably even among the vision statement writers. In the
years since the release of that statement, I have certainly seen even
greater variance in commitment to equity among the organizers and
implementers of PDSs across the country. As I have read about, vis-
ited, and talked to people involved in PDSs, I have definitely noticed
what Murrell describes as the differences between the "espoused" and
the "real"—the distinction between the PDS concept and the "movement." In some PDS settings, little more than lip service has been given
to the importance of equity. Even where commitment has been deep
and understanding thorough, I have seen PDS partners' inability to
discuss tough issues with each other lead to a "plateau" effect, where
deep-seated goals like equity take a back seat to more immediately
achievable goals like setting up clusters of student teacher placements
in a school (Teitel, 1998).

On the other hand, professional development schools are part of a
many- splendored movement, with a huge range of partnerships identifying themselves as PDSs, and no set of standards yet in place to
determine which is "worthy of the name" (Sykes, 1997). So, when
Murrell paints with a broad brush to note that all PDSs are formally
structured in ways that exclude community members, there will be
some readers (myself among them) who will contest, by power of
counter-example, his more sweeping statements. Similarly, contrary
to Murrell's repeated assertion, there are urban schools that have ben-
efited a great deal from being a PDS.

These disagreements do not undermine Murrell's major point, or
the real contribution that this monograph makes. It refocuses us, in
very concrete ways, on a major part of what brought us to see PDSs as
a way to simultaneously improve schools and colleges. Murrell, in his
cogently argued way, forces us to keep our eyes on the prize. For this,
we owe him and this monograph a major debt of thanks. This work
will be a significant tool for advocates and insiders to raise issues that
have otherwise remained largely unspoken. It challenges theorists to
look at PDS organizational structures and see which aspects inhibit
the true goals of PDSs, as Murrell suggests. It throws down the gaunt-
let to PDS advocates to challenge Murrell's assertions about the failure of PDSs to impact urban schools. It will be a powerful aid for funding agencies and networks to refocus and redouble efforts that put

student learning, social justice, and equity back on the front burner and in so doing, will help us all keep our eyes on the prize—and hold on.

Lee Teitel
University of Massachusetts-Boston
April 1998

References

Sykes, G. (1997). Worthy of the Name: Standards for Professional Development Schools. In M. Levine and R. Trachtman (Eds.), <u>Building professional development schools: Politics, practice and policy</u> (pp. 159-181). New York: Teachers College Press.

Teitel, L. (1998). Changing teacher education through professional development school partnerships: A five year follow-up study. Teachers College Record.

Valli, L., Cooper, D., and Frankes, L. (1997). Professional development schools and equity: A critical analysis of rhetoric and research. In M. W. Apple (Ed.), <u>Review of research in education,</u> 22, 251-304. Washington, DC: American Educational Research Association.

ABOUT THE AUTHOR

Peter Murrell is an Associate Professor of Urban Education at Northeastern University, where he is also the Director of the Master of Arts in Teaching Program in the Center for Innovation in Urban Education. He received his Ph.D. in Urban Education-Educational Psychology from the University of Wisconsin-Milwaukee, specializing in human learning and cognition. He earned his M.S. degree from the University of Wisconsin-Madison in Experimental Psychology specializing in cognition and learning, and his B.A. in Psychology from Carleton College in Northfield, Minnesota.

A consultant to schools and school systems in the areas of learning environments, urban pedagogy (teaching and learning in diverse settings), assessment and program evaluation, he also has served as a member of national invited study groups such as the Carnegie Foundation study group on Interdisciplinary Middle School Curriculum, and the Office of Educational Research and Improvement (U.S. Department of Education) study group on World Class Standard and Teacher Education.

Dr. Murrell's research is in the area of qualitative studies of human learning and cognition in cultural and community context. His current research focuses on how academic achievement and proficiencies can be promoted through experiential and service-learning relationships between universities and urban communities.

INTRODUCTION

The idea of the Professional Development School (PDS) has taken center stage in school reform movements in recent years. The concept has emerged in a number of venues (e.g., Darling-Hammond, 1992; Darling-Hammond, Lieberman, McLauglin, and Miller, 1992; Goodlad, 1988, 1994; Lieberman and Miller, 1990; Holmes Group, 1986b, 1990; The Carnegie Forum, 1986). Essentially, a PDS is an elementary, middle, or high school in which school people and university people have agreed to work cooperatively to develop the capacities of all educators associated with the school. This includes both university faculty and classroom teachers, who work toward mutually-determined common goals for improving educational outcomes for the students in the school.

Increasingly, the PDS movement is being regarded as an engine of school reform nationwide (cf. Report of the National Commission on Teaching & America's Future [NCTAF], 1996), from which new models of teacher education, professional development, and innovative instruction are expected to emerge. Advocacy for the model is strongly linked with the national movements toward standards, accountability, and the professionalization of teaching. However, as Zeichner (1996) points out, the role of teacher education that has been overlooked in proposals to close the so-called "achievement gap" in urban schools in the past has now surfaced in problematic form (p. 67).

PDS advocacy for urban school reform often implies that the task for teacher education is a simple matter of identifying the right teaching and curriculum practices for effective work in urban contexts, so that the *solution* to urban under-achievement is the *training* of teachers to use these practices. Zeichner (1996) states that simply putting new teaching technology into the hands of a culturally-encapsulated, largely white, monolingual corps of teachers makes no difference in their effectiveness unless their professional development forces them to confront how they view themselves as cultural beings with respect to poor students of color (p. 67).

The authors of the NCTAF Report, *What Matters Most,* and other PDS advocates are right to call for the professional development and preparation of teachers as central to addressing issues of achievement and development in urban schools (e.g., the so-called "urban achievement gap," Williams, 1996). But they are wrong to suggest, given the current configuration of public school policy and the cultural values of schooling in America, that we can synthesize and standardize effective teaching practice in diverse urban communities through PDS training of teachers. Unless the assumptions, attitudes, and cultural boundedness of teachers are central to teacher education, no amount of professional development will make a difference in the quality of urban schools.

Popular ideas, such as the notion of the Professional Development School, represent both opportunity and danger to budding initiatives for renewing urban schools and communities. The opportunity aspect appears often in the advocacy and research literature on PDSs, but the optimism for productive work in urban schools is not supported by evidence. The danger of the PDS idea lies in that optimism. The danger is, in the complex work of community mobilization and educational development in urban communities, an idea like PDS may be appropriated in ways that ultimately prove destructive to the goals of equity, quality education, and justice.

Despite the growing interest and popularity of the PDS idea, there has been little evidence demonstrating positive impact on schooling in culturally, racially, and linguistically diverse urban communities. Although equity was an original focus of the PDS movement, according to the Holmes Group (1986b), PDS approaches have yielded few tangible results with respect to effective work in diverse urban schools and communities. Why has the PDS movement, ostensibly dedicated to improving teaching and learning in under-resourced, diverse urban communities, generally failed at this effort? This question is examined by using a critical analysis to propose future directions for the role of the professional development school agenda in urban communities.

This monograph is not simply a critique of the PDS model, nor of the PDS movement, it is intended to inform the decision making and planning of those truly dedicated to the development of children in racially, culturally, and linguistically diverse urban communities who may be embarking on a partnership venture. It is an analytic survey of the PDS concept as it applies to improving urban schools and teacher preparation. In particular, the problematic application of the PDS idea to improving teaching practice for effective work in culturally, racially, and linguistically diverse urban schools will be examined. I take the position that, although the PDS idea represents an early innovation in teacher education, the PDS concept has limited application to successful work in diverse urban communities.

"It's All in the Knowing How!"

As I worked to make this perspective clear in the final preparation of this manuscript, I looked again at the set of articles reporting on the benefits of PDSs in urban contexts—exemplars of PDSs that "were working" to close the achievement gap in urban schools. I realized that every aspect that writers reported as a positive outcome of the PDS did not result from the PDS structure, but rather was the result of what people *did with*, and *added to*, that structure. It occurred to me then that the problem of evaluating the PDS idea, with respect to effective work in urban schools, is like stone soup. Let me elaborate with that children's story (Brown, 1947).

This story is set in a time gone by in a place far away and finds three soldiers trudging down a road in an unfamiliar country. Coming home from the wars, they were tired and very hungry having eaten nothing in two days. As they approached a village, the villagers saw them coming and began talking worriedly among themselves. Fearing that they would have to share meager food resources with the newcomers, they set about hiding their vegetables and other foodstuffs. As the soldiers stopped at each house to ask for a bit of food, they met with the same response time and again. They were denied with excuses: "We have had no food for ourselves for three days," or "It has been a poor harvest," or "We gave all we could spare to soldiers who came before you." And, so it went as the three soldiers went from cottage to cottage. The villagers stood in the street, sighing and looking as hungry as they could.

The three soldiers put their heads together and developed a plan. One of the soldiers cried out to the villagers, drawing them near, "Good people! We are three hungry soldiers in a strange land. We have asked you for food, and you have no food. Well then, we'll have to make stone soup." Now *this* was something the villagers had to see. They milled around as their curiosity overcame their self interest. "First we'll need a large iron pot," the soldiers said. The peasants brought the largest pot they could find. The soldiers said, "And now, water to fill it and a fire to heat it," to which the villagers complied by filling the pot and then building the fire. The soldiers said, "And now, if you please, three round, smooth stones." The villagers watched in amazement as the soldiers began stirring the pot.

"Any soup needs salt and pepper," said the soldiers, and children ran to get them. "Stones like these generally make good soup, but oh, if there were carrots, it would be much better," said the soldiers. A village woman, who thought she *just might* have a carrot or two returned with an apron-full of carrots she had hidden as the soldiers entered the village. "A good stone soup should have cabbage," said the soldiers, "but no use asking for what you don't have." A villager woman who thought she might be able to locate one, came with three she had hidden. And so it went. Each ingredient that the soldiers suggested might make the soup just that much better, the villagers managed to find. A "bit" of beef, a "few" potatoes, a "little" barley, and a cup of milk resulted, of course, in the most magnificent soup. When the soup was ready, the "taste" offered the villagers evolved into feast and festivity far into the night.

What lessons are illustrated in the analogy? First, a PDS is like the beginnings of stone soup. A PDS offers the potential of a desired result—an effective school—just as stone soup offers the potential of a tasty meal. But clearly, much more needs to happen to reach that end. Creating an effective urban PDS, like making stone soup, is always a value-added enterprise. When the soldiers dropped in the stones, they did not yet have a meal, but beginning elements essential to that meal— a pot and hot water. Second, whether building a quality school or making stone soup, the outcome depends on the processes of participation, and drawing everyone in who needs to be at the table, figuratively and literally. And, maybe, just maybe, you need an inducement, whether it is the curiosity of creating a soup from stones or the status of being a PDS. Third, there is a lesson about how one enters into community with others. While some might see the cleverness of the soldiers as trickery or deceit, others may simply recognize "know how"—how to elicit participation and a community sensibility. After all, the villagers did nothing against their will, and the flow of events elicited their generous and humane natures.

Finally, asking whether PDSs "work" for children in diverse urban communities is the wrong question—not because the PDS framework is without merit, but because the question is irrelevant. It is like asking whether stone soup is nourishing. The quality of a professional development school, like the quality of stone soup, depends upon who participates and what they "put into the mix." The lesson is not just about the importance of eliciting participation, but, more importantly, not mistaking the beginning elements of the stone soup or the PDS for the feast that is the quality school community. As the soldiers remarked upon leaving the village after the feast and a fond farewell, "Oh, it's all in the knowing how!"

Monograph Overview

Like the making of stone soup, the process of developing a working collaborative in a school is what determines success. What goes into the process—the "knowing how" portion of elevating children's achievement and development in urban schools—is complex. Two features distinguish this monograph from prior writing on the PDS model. First, what follows is a critical analysis of the theoretical foundations of the PDS idea in relation to teacher preparation, school improvement, and community development in culturally, linguistically, and racially diverse urban contexts. This analytic survey will provide a structural analysis of the PDS model and an assessment of its value for effective work in diverse urban schools and communities.

Second, the analysis disentangles the *PDS concept* from the *PDS movement*. There are essentially two literatures on PDSs—a research literature corresponding to the development and application of the PDS concept, and an advocacy literature corresponding to policy regarding the PDS concept. This monograph examines the PDS model on both of these counts to provide a systematic means of addressing the discontinuities between theory and practice and between practices and policies in PDS work as it applies to urban schools and communities.

This analytic survey is organized into three chapters. The first clarifies what is meant by the PDS model and describes the central goals of PDS initiatives. Chapter two critically assesses the value of the PDS idea to school renewal and the preparation of teachers for effective work in diverse urban schools and communities. It addresses the essential question of why the PDS framework is insufficient for effective, quality educational practice in diverse urban communities and critically reinterprets the notion of the professional development school in light of the critical knowledge required for successful work in diverse urban contexts (e.g., Cochran-Smith, 1997; Hilliard, 1997; Irvine, 1997; Melnick & Zeichner, 1997; Murrell & Diez, 1997; Murrell, 1994; Zeichner, 1996). A summary of problems related to applying the PDS framework to work in urban education is included.

Chapter three explores alternative approaches for collaborative teacher preparation, professional development, and school renewal in diverse urban settings. This monograph concludes with a conceptual framework summarizing the features required for an equity-minded, urban-focused, and diversity-responsive type of collaborative approach to university-school partnerships.

1
THE PROFESSIONAL
DEVELOPMENT SCHOOL CONCEPT

In basic terms, the PDS is a form of collaborative partnership between a university's school of education and a P-12 school. The primary aim is to improve teaching on two levels by providing a rich, collaborative, inquiry-based school site within which clinical preparation of preservice teachers takes place; and providing a collegial context for teacher educators and experienced teachers to collaborate on the improvement of teaching practice in the school. Valli, Cooper, and Frankes (1997) adopt the Holmes Group (1990) definition of a PDS: a professional development school is a "school for the development of novice professionals, for continuing development of experienced professionals and *for the research and development of the teaching profession*" [emphasis added] (p. 1). A PDS partnership must be "systematically and simultaneously engaged in teacher preparation, professional development, and research on a school-wide basis" to be considered a PDS (Valli et al., 1997, p. 252).

A professional development school builds on the historical and traditional connection between schools of education and the P-12 schools. This consists of what I call the clinical triad—involving a teacher educator (university supervisor), a field-based educator (cooperating teacher), and a novice teacher (student teacher or intern). The basic activity setting is one in which the teacher educator and cooperating teacher collaboratively assist the development of the novice teacher through observations, joint conferences, and assigned tasks. To this basic relationship, the PDS adds the prospect of collaborative work between university teacher educators, experienced teachers, and other school-based personnel. Therefore, this definition of a PDS excludes affiliative partnership arrangements between P-12 schools and universities that focus only on inservice teachers or only on preservice teacher preparation.

The intent of the PDS idea is to build a *community of practice* (Lave, 1988, 1997) that is broader and more inclusive of the basic clinical triad described above (see also, Lemke, 1997; Walkerdine, 1997). This means the development of an enclave of practitioners who work together to more fully understand the culture of the school and the interrelation of activity systems within the school. A community of practice focuses on developing practices for improving teaching and learning according to a specific vision of change. Thus, the concept of the PDS would exclude collaborations among groups of teachers and teacher educators whose research and professional development activities were not organized by a formal PDS institutional agreement. Finally, this definition excludes affiliative school-university arrangements for which there is not an institutional commitment to a particular vision of change (see, for example, the National Center for Restructuring Education, Schools and Teaching [NCREST] vision, 1993).

In the PDS advocacy and research literature, the term PDS may denote either the partnership between university and school collaborators or the school itself. However, professional development schools are actual P-12 schools. The schools may be elementary, middle, or high schools, but in all cases they constitute the setting for the university-school collaboration. PDSs are often public schools, although some PDSs are also parochial, pilot schools, and charter schools (Abdal-Haqq, 1996). This last feature is significant, since it is the public nature that distinguishes PDSs from one of its chief precursors, the laboratory school, whereby a university runs a school as a laboratory of good practice that is usually populated by the offspring of the university faculty members.

Finally, PDSs are always some kind of collaborative affiliation or partnership, whether they include other constituents (e.g., school boards, corporate partners, and community agency partners) or not. PDSs *as schools* are presumed to be in the process of becoming exemplary schools. PDSs *as partnerships* are presumed to make the process happen. These presumptions are examples of the excess of the PDS advocacy literature.

The Purposes of PDSs

The first report of the Holmes Group (1986b), *Tomorrow's Teachers*, coined the term professional development school in one of the first attempts to articulate a conception of *in situ* professional development of teachers and school improvement beyond that of the old lab school concept. In the past, the lab school concept prevailed, where the university-owned school provided both personnel and material resources that made them exceptional places for innovation, but limited in its applicability to wider agendas of reform and renewal. As both Hargreaves (1995, p. 29) and Sarason (1993, pp. 26-27) explain, this type of PDS could, at best, illustrate how to create a new school, but not how to reform and renew an existing one. The new idea was that professional development schools would be exemplary practicum sites needed to provide teachers-in-preparation rich, cutting-edge clinical experience in schools organized according to the best available knowledge about teaching. This idea is nicely articulated by Judge, Carriedo, and Johnson (1995):

> The PDS is to be, first and foremost, a partnership and not a colonizing effort by the university; it is to bring to bear the capacities and resources of higher education upon the resolution of urgent practical problems encountered in the public schools and the society in which they are embedded; it is to establish a new if uncomfortable relationship between research and practice; and...it is to be a critically important base for the preparation of future educators (section 4).

According to Abdal-Haqq (1996) and the data collected by the Clinical Schools Clearinghouse, there are currently an estimated 650 professional development schools in the United States. Following Abdal-Haqq's (1997) characterization of the purposes of the professional development school, the following four purposes serve as criteria for determining whether a collaborative partnership is a PDS:

- the preparation of teachers and other school-based educators;
- the professional development of practicing (i.e., experienced) teachers and other school-based educators;
- the focus on development of exemplary instructional and educational experiences for students; and
- the applied inquiry (e.g., action research) designed to improve practice. (p. viii)

Abdal-Haqq (1998) also notes that not every school can or should be a PDS, but every PDS ought to collaborate with a university towards improving teaching and learning at the school (p. 6). Too often, this important idea is overlooked. Clearly, becoming a PDS does not automatically imply fruitful innovation in teaching or enhanced clinical preparation of teachers.

The Vision of the PDS Movement

PDS advocates articulate the model as a system of school reform. On this account, the PDS is regarded as a special case of school restructuring, whereby new models of teacher education, professional development, innovative instruction, and program building are the outcomes of the collaboration. Moreover, on this account the PDS stimulates simultaneous institutional transformation in both the school and university contexts (e.g., Darling-Hammond, 1992; Goodlad, 1988, 1991, 1994; Holmes Group, 1986a, 1986b, 1990; The Carnegie Forum, 1986). Goals for PDSs put forward by NCREST (1993) represents the vision in the following points:

■ Centering schools on learners and learning—PDSs should develop a shared, publicly articulated vision and commitment to a set of core beliefs that apply to all learners;

■ Communication and collaboration—Teaching and learning are not isolated work. They require many opportunities for communication and collaboration among learners—adults and children;

■ Connection and community—Since individuals learn more effectively when they learn together, communities of learners must be forged within schools and across traditional school/community boundaries;

■ Commitment to developing knowledge and promoting inquiry—Members of the PDS community are engaged in systematic, collaborative, and continuous inquiry about teaching and learning;

■ Shared responsibility for the learning of all members of the PDS community—Everyone on the joint school and university faculty assumes a collective professional responsibility for the welfare of all learners (students, novice teachers, veteran teachers, teacher educators, administrators);

■   Parity in partnerships—PDS partnerships are forged
    with a commitment to mutual trust, respect, and par-
    ity resulting in reciprocity and collective ownership
    of the enterprise;

■   Continual renewal and improvement—The PDS as an
    organization and members of the PDS community are
    committed to continual reflection, self and organiza-
    tional renewal, and the pursuit of ever more power-
    ful and inclusive approaches to supporting student
    success. (pp. 3-4)

In summary, the PDS at its essence is a particular type of institutional organization founded on the basic university-school bilateral
cooperative relationship for teacher preparation. The working part of
the PDS is the development of a community of practice that expands
upon the basic clinical triad in teacher preparation to include other
teachers and a broader agenda than teacher preparation. The addi-
tional defining features of a PDS are the four criteria given by Abdal-
Haqq (1997) and the vision of school change in the seven NCREST
(1993) principles. It is important to note that nothing in these defining
features specifically relates to the central issues and concerns of urban
schools in diverse communities.

2
PROBLEMS OF THE PDS MODEL
IN URBAN SCHOOLS

Our comprehensive review of the research indicates that PDS achievements still fall short of expectations. In many instances, instrumental recommendations about linking theory to practice, strengthening school-university collaboration, and providing time for professional development seem to have become ends in themselves. Or they are linked to commonly accepted [not innovative] notions of higher achievement for students and teacher candidates. While there is some commitment to establishing PDSs in inner cities, broad issues of equity and social justice are often absent in both PDS research and practice. (Valli et al., 1997, p. 252)

The promise that the PDS model will help transform public schools into multicultural, democratic learning communities has not been realized (Murrell & Borunda, 1997). In the decade since its inception, the PDS movement has failed to live up to the promise of ameliorating inequalities in the learning environments of children in urban public schools even though the PDS concept in its many articulations (Holmes Group, 1986b, 1990; Darling-Hammond, 1994) espouses a commitment to educational equity. There is painfully little evidence of this commitment in either the PDS advocacy literature or the PDS research literature (cf. Valli et al., 1997; Teitel, 1996).

Many political, economic, social, and technological forces are pressuring schools to restructure so they serve all students better. There is significant evidence, however, that generic restructuring of frameworks and designs will not change urban schools. The generic frameworks and designs do not pay sufficient attention to the unique issues and conditions that these schools must confront every day (Williams, 1996, p. 2).

PDS advocates have hailed the PDS model as the engine of urban school reform, capable of transforming schools into places "...where teachers can learn from each other ..." and where "...children will learn more..." (Holmes Group, 1986b, p. 4). The system of relationships organized by a PDS is problematic in two ways. First, PDSs are ostensibly organized to facilitate the learning of children. Yet, the organizational structures of PDSs are geared to the "tooling up" of teachers with little or no evidence of commensurate design for the development of children. Second, although the PDS idea is touted as a movement to benefit the most under-served schools and communities, it is, in fact, a movement ostensibly driven by the same American myths that historically have been destructive to the interests of people of color. Comer (1997) identifies two of these as meritocracy myths: (1) the belief that an individual's life outcomes are due almost entirely to genetically determined intelligence and will; and (2) that whites have been more successful than blacks, and blacks, therefore, merit less (pp. 4-6).

Although there is significant educational literature produced by African American scholars, as well as other people of color, that exposes the cultural values in American society destructive to public education in diverse communities, PDS work seems not to access this literature at all. These myths persist unabated, even in PDSs thought to be "working." The critical meta-issues of public schooling in American education that the PDS movement is designed to address—issues of power, equity, privilege, and community building—are precisely those which remain congenitally inaccessible to institutions structured as PDSs.

In particular, there appears to be no systematic examination in the PDS literature of critical perspectives on racism and white privilege and how these are implicated in the sort-and-select practices of standardized testing and tracking. Further, there is no evidence in the PDS research literature regarding the issues of exclusion, educational inequality, or community development. These are essential considerations for work in diverse urban schools and communities and ought to be the leading edge of PDS work.

The evidence to date (e.g., Valli et al., 1997; Teitel, 1996) suggests that without significant re-examination of the PDS patterns of institutional organization and practices, any extension of the PDS model will pave over, not repair, the fatal flaws in the foundations of urban schooling. The more appropriate metaphor for PDS work at this point is not the *leading edge* of innovative and improved practice, but rather the *shroud* which hides, and perhaps perpetuates, fundamental problems and issues from the light of critical inspection.

PDS as an organizational structure is politically, ideologically, and culturally neutral with respect to its constituency in urban communities—a fact that virtually guarantees its failure in those contexts. How will a PDS allow for a critical exploration of equity when no such agenda or consciousness exists? How can the organizational structure of a PDS lead to community building when the roles of the leading "players" are prescribed? How can a PDS build a community of practice within an organizational structure that inhibits conversations necessary for building democratic participation? What possibility is there for a PDS collaborative to become a "democratic public sphere" (Giroux, 1992, p. 5), given the congenital asymmetries of power that leave parents and community stakeholders out of the equation? How can PDS partnerships deal responsively and democratically with wider constituencies of parents and community stakeholders when the design categorically excludes them?

These are serious questions given the scarcity of evidence that they are part of the discourse of inquiry in PDSs. The seriousness of this absence of discourse in the PDS research literature is compounded by the fact that no systematic reform agenda in regard to issues of equity, power, and diversity exists. This is due, in part to the inescapable and troublesome asymmetries in power—the structuring of activities in PDS affiliations inevitably privileges professionals.

Why the PDS Concept Isn't Working

Why is the PDS program inadequate to bring out effective teacher preparation and school development in diverse urban communities? The reasons are rooted in four problems:

1. PDSs are not designed, and thereby inhibit, the questioning of the underlying political questions and socio-cultural dynamics that produce inequities in schooling;

2. The PDS framework, as it currently exists, inhibits the development of conceptually rich, culturally aware, and politically astute definitions of equity, diversity, and quality schooling;

3. The PDS organizational framework maintains the political status quo by failing to address real needs, interests, and agendas of urban communities supposedly served by PDSs, and;

4. Due to the disconnectedness of the PDS organizational struc-
    ture from the wider community, theoretical frameworks for
    pedagogical inquiry are inadequate.

It is important at this juncture to offer two caveats. The first is to
acknowledge a simple yet important reality—that the PDS is simply a
type of collaborative affiliation driven by mutual concerns in teacher
preparation, innovation of practices, and professional development.
No one can deny the value of an arrangement whereby university
educators seek to situate their programs of professional training and
knowledge production in the real contexts. Nor can anyone can deny
the value of enlisting the participation of school personnel towards
these ends. In short, if you want to make soup it is good to have a pot
and boiling water.

Neither can anyone question the positive changes that professional
development schools have brought into teacher education. The pre-
cepts of PDS work, as articulated by NCREST (1993) constitute a powerful and important guide for practice. However, once we acknowledge the undisputed value of school-university partnership in general, and the contributions of the PDS idea in particular, it is important to confront the question as to whether the PDS institutional organization is the most appropriate for the future critical work to be done
in urban schools.

The point of being explicit about this caveat is to recognize the
polysemy of the PDS idea. In the popular, advocacy, and research literature regarding PDSs, there appears to be at least three categories of
meaning for the term: (1) PDS as synonymous with partnership; (2)
PDS as synonymous with a particular type of partnership between
school and university partners; and (3) PDS as the school itself, including its enacted organizational structure. Henceforth in this analysis, PDS connotes categories two and three, defining the pattern of
relationships and organizational structure—both the theorized and
enacted—in the professional development school.

The second caveat is to acknowledge that what a PDS actually
becomes is largely shaped by factors beyond the control of its organizers, designers, and advocates—and this is especially true if it is
done democratically. On one level, the meso level of analysis, this means
that, as soldiers entering a village, we do not know in advance what it
will take to make a feast out of stone soup. On another level, the macro
level of analysis, this means that the PDS structure owes its existence as
much to how society already organizes its educational institutions as
much as it does to the creative capacity of educational thinkers.

Public culture and prevailing governmental policy play a huge role in the social, political, cultural, and fiscal organization of PDSs. In this sense, PDSs are not new inventions as much as they are rebuilt machinery from an earlier era, necessarily constrained by what came before, the earlier machinery being the laboratory school. This constraint tends to lock out other ways of organizing schools for improved teaching and learning. I call this idea the "institutional boundedness" of PDSs; an idea to which I will return.

Problem One—Political Status Quo Regarding Problems of Urban Schooling

It is beyond dispute that public schooling in America is a socializing force recreating social stratification in American society. American educators have been very slow to recognize the role schooling plays in maintaining and replicating an undemocratic, hierarchical social order—reproducing disparities of wealth, cultural dominance, and unequal political relationships between groups and classes (cf. Bordieu & Passeron, 1977; Bowles & Gintes, 1976; Freire, 1993; Woodson, 1933/1990). It is therefore imperative, given the cultural and racial politics of American schooling, that educational advocacy on behalf of children of color be capable of critically interrogating the institutions, foundations, and practices of the status quo.

Advocates for children in beleaguered urban public schools must be fundamentally subversive at particular junctures where the interests of children are opposed by the interests of reform agendas and schooling bureaucracies (Murrell, 1997). This means, for example, that university people may need, at times, to take stances that oppose the interests of the school partners and school bureaucracies—such as instituting a program of standardized testing that is destined to ruin any opportunity for a coherent, rich curriculum—if they truly advocate for the educational quality of children. More importantly, both university and school professionals may need to stand back as people advocate for themselves and their children's education.

From the perspective of communities of color, the sort-and-select, meritocracy system of education in the United States must be continuously interrogated and contested. This necessary critical interrogation is rare in educational discourse, and rarer still in the development of PDS relationships. Thanks to the work of writers like Samuel Bowles and Herbert Gintes, Paulo Freire, Pierre Bordieu, and Henry Giroux, more educators have come to understand that the American educational system was designed to produce winners and losers. The system that works so well for those with the appropriate "cultural capital" also works well in relegating the poor and children of color to the lower realms of a social order.

The PDS literature reveals no critique of the sort-and-select, meritocracy system of education—a critique that is essential to building an equity agenda and quality community schooling in diverse urban contexts. Similarly, there is no substantive PDS critique of the meritocracy ideology of the American system of education that is designed to differentiate children. The problem is that the PDS movement is cut from the same ideological cloth as the system that must have "losers" by design.

Here is an example of this political status quo at work. In the PDS advocacy literature (e.g., Darling-Hammond, 1994), the analogy between the PDS and the teaching hospital in the medical profession is often drawn. The analogy breaks down at a critical point—the "knowing how" of building a community. A teaching hospital is not a model for building a collaborative partnership across boundaries of class, race, culture, and professional privilege as is required in creating a PDS. In a teaching hospital, inflexible, linear, top-down, and directive chains-of-command are more typical of the relationships among the professionals, and between professionals and clients. In that social system, it is abundantly clear who dictates terms and who gets dictated to. Patients have next to nothing to say about professional judgments regarding their treatment and care. They take their medicine and follow their medical regimen. From the perspective of those urban educators knowledgeable about community building and collaboration, this system of relationships is *not* acceptable nor is the teaching hospital system of relationships consistent with the vision for the good school as articulated in the NCREST (1993) PDS vision principles previously listed.

Educators who recognize the importance of improving the teaching profession will undoubtedly find the "teaching hospital" analogy compelling. However, the analogy skirts over the critical issues of power and cultural hegemony and fortifies the political neutrality of the PDS idea. A different conception, more appropriate to collaboration in successful urban schools, is that of the community of practice (Lave, 1988, 1997; Lemke, 1997; Walkerdine, 1997). To develop a school as a community of practice would mean that every member would be continuously and interactively occupied with the quality of learning in the school. It would also mean that the membership would not be limited to teacher educators and teachers. Rather than instituting a structure, as is the case with the typical PDS approach, the primary focus of the collaborative would be developing a deep understanding of how children learn, develop, and achieve.

A number of writers offer important critiques (e.g., Myers, 1996b; Labaree & Pallas, 1996; Valli, 1994) and significant reformulations of the PDS idea including professional learning communities (Myers, 1996b); professional development teams (Schack & Overturf, 1994); and empowering learning communities (Valli, 1994). Valli (1994) offers a vision of the PDS as "an empowering, emancipating learning community that frees people from trivial knowledge as well as ignorance." But beyond the ability to articulate an appealing vision of what PDSs should look like, and beyond the development of theory that unifies the vision and with the practice, there is another quality which Meier (1982) termed "the humility of good anthropology" (p. 14).

This idea relates to whether university educators, teachers and other school professionals can adopt the respectful stance necessary to fully access the local pedagogical understanding and knowledge of the communities they enter. PDS practice provides no context to develop this "humility of good anthropology." In the university classroom or in the PDS planning team meeting, deliberation over essential questions like "What are schools for?" or "What kind of learning community do we want?" have a starting-from-scratch quality that contrasts with the urgency experienced by parents and children in diverse urban communities served by public schools. The point is considerations such as caring, problem-solving, respecting differences, and resisting hegemony (Valli, 1994) are not "start-from-scratch" considerations in the way PDS participants might engage them in seminar discussion or planning sessions. Respect for language and culture is not a "start-from-scratch" proposition from the perspective of parents whose children attend the beleaguered and under-resourced schools found in so many urban school districts.

From a community perspective, there is not the hesitation of scholarly reflection when a "poverty of pedagogy" is a pressing reality of the school your child attends. There is an impatience with consensus building, mission statement writing, or values clarification when the total failure of a school is at hand. From a community perspective, the urgency of the disproportionate expulsion and suspension of African American and Latino children points to obvious answers to the question: "What kind of learning community do we want?" From the perspective of parents and children who suffer the consequences of public schools' failure, where to begin on school renewal is not a matter that requires a lot of scholarly deliberation. It is the reality of the distance between bureaucratic institutions and real communities that torpedoes the equity agenda of the PDS schools (Murrell & Borunda, 1997).

Problem Two—Who Gets Left Out?
Casualties of the PDS Institutional Structure

There is a way in which the bilateral reorganization of a school by two polarities—university and school people—has a chilling and distancing effect on the participation of parents and community stakeholders. Myers (1996a) concludes:

> The analysis shows that the partnership efforts that were studied (and probably partnership and PDS efforts in general) devote significantly less attention to ideas about the nature of schools, learning, teaching, the knowledge base for teaching, and teacher learning and professional development than the attention they devote to establishing university-school arrangements, to the mechanics of operation, and to the interpersonal relationships involved in bringing in university teacher educators and pre-K-12 teachers together. The main focus of nearly all efforts is inducting new teachers into schools. Little attention is devoted to helping university teacher educators or experienced pre-K-12 school faculty study their own practice, improve their work, or reform what they do. (p. 1)

PDS organizational structures operate from the sanctity of the professional domain which *includes* teachers, professors, and school-based personnel, but *excludes* parents and other non-professional members of the school community. PDS institutional structure obscures the fact that not all the work for improving the lives and learning achievement of children is "professional." It is unclear how those situated in a PDS structure can circumvent this limitation as there are few, if any, compelling examples in the literature of this occurring. There are at least five internal power-organizational issues of the PDS bilateral structure as well, that involve the inescapable problems of determining participation.

First, although only a few PDS studies explicitly look at this issue of participation (e.g., Teitel, 1997), it is clear that there is always someone marginalized at the start-up of a PDS partnership. Despite attempts at creating fair means of deciding who participates (e.g., selecting from among those who indicate interest or voting for participants), there is an inevitable exclusion and subsequent marginalization because not everyone can be a player in the "PDS game." Not every teacher in a new PDS can work in the collaborative.

Secondly, the organizational structure seems to dictate function in the PDS organizational structure. Categories of membership and hierarchical participation structures are determined before the purposes, the value, or the risks of the enterprise are fully apparent to people in the setting. This restricts access to their meaningful participation which is, in any event, ad hoc. Thoughtful observers have articulated this problem of structure preceding purpose (e.g., Diez in Ponessa, 1997) and have expressed concern that instituting the PDS organizational structure may needlessly limit a partnership's capacity for effective work. Diez notes, "Structure is simply too narrow of a beginning focus and cuts off other possibilities. I think people have gotten stuck in what they think is the recipe from on high" (Ponessa, 1997, p. 5).

Many important educational issues such as curriculum standards, high-stakes testing, and student achievement are more successfully addressed in a collective, community-mobilized school development effort that include the "consumers" of public education (Wagner, 1995, 1997). Productive change in urban schools requires a much broader array of activity settings than the *clinical triad*—which is the most prevalent and institutionalized *activity setting* in professional development schools. Structuring the collaborative as an enclave of professionals (i.e., teachers and university people), instead of predicating structure on a problem to be solved or a movement to be energized, will continue to privilege professionalism above the interests of the community.

A third aspect of the internal power issues in the bilateral organization of PDS concerns how unexamined power relations damage the capacity for effective team work. I refer here to *disguised authority*—embedded power relations that go uninterrogated but that nonetheless subvert movement toward more democratic forms of school life. There will always be inherent structural features of the PDS that subvert attempts to equalize power. For example, Valli et al., (1997) examines the PDS idea of a *hand-over of authority*. One inherent problem is that to complete a process of hand-over is to claim power and admit hegemony—and these may not have been seriously questioned or discussed among those in the collaborative. Power equalization falls far short of democratization. If it did not, other people besides the university and school polarities would be involved; and from Freire's (1970/1993) perspective, participants would see just how undemocratic and patronizing a "transfer of authority" project really is.

A fourth problem with the PDS bilateral organizational structure concerns the way in which the sanctum of professionals—university faculty, teacher educators and field based instructors—constitute a "culture of power" (Delpit, 1988) within the PDS community. This culture resists attempts to mitigate the hierarchical relationships which ensue. Valli et al. (1997) suggest that "A tighter coupling of university and school is accomplished through 'blurring boundaries' that traditionally have separated the two institutions" (p. 22). I submit that such blurring tends to lock out other participants in a needed rupturing of those boundaries and the hegemony they preserve.

For example, when university professors in a meeting with teachers and parents declare that they are "not the experts" and "everyone is an equal in the conversation" they have merely disguised the fact that their perspective carries more weight by virtue of their assumed expertise. Egalitarian relationships do not occur simply by the declaration of the more powerful party. This is precisely analogous to Delpit's (1988) observation of how the obfuscation of power on the part of progressive educators exacerbates the marginalization of black children and their parents. The same happens in PDSs, only in this case, the marginalized are the non-PDS players in the school, along with parents of color.

The fifth problem with the bilateral PDS structure concerns the organization of activity. Because of the limitation of roles people can take in the PDS structure, there is a greater danger of intensification (Hargreaves, 1994, pp. 14-15). This means that rather than collective reflection on practice, teachers become wrapped up in taking on many more roles. Valli et al. (1997) describes intensification in PDSs:

> Too many additional responsibilities may ultimately lead to greater disempowerment and isolation of teachers. Working as members of site-based management teams, as student teacher supervisors, and as university-school liaisons may detract from teachers' ability to fully perform their critical role as classroom teachers. (p. 273)

Thus, this kind of intensification of teacher work may be falsely construed as increasing professional autonomy and somehow benefiting children and youth.

Problem Three—Organizing PDSs
Lessons Learned from Michigan State University

The processes and activities surrounding the institution of a PDS too often leave out the real needs, interests, and agendas of people in the diverse urban communities that the school partnership is supposed to serve. There are many alternatives to organizing urban schools initiatives, including networks, teaching collaboratives, and true community building as exemplified by the work of James Comer (1997). These approaches are less institutionally bounded because they are trans-institutional, that is, involving a multiplicity of schools and institutions of higher education where the focus is on a specific population of children. The interests and needs of people supersede the interests of formalizing agreements, and in fact are the basis of organizing the work of the institutions.

The critical mistake that is repeated time and again in PDS start-ups is that professional educators think they can constitute a new culture and a new community without the participation from the culture and community that already exists. Comparison of the PDS approach to these alternate models is not the interest here (see, Lawson, 1996). This section examines more closely the process of realizing a PDS in relation to the issues of quality education in urban contexts.

Michigan State University (MSU) engaged in a major, multi-school PDS initiative as part of the Michigan Partnership for New Education (MPNE), out of which, arguably, much of the PDS movement has grown. In summarizing the lessons from PDSs in urban schools, it will be instructive here to draw on some conclusions resulting from a systemic internal review by MSU. The review revealed:

1. Although the Michigan Partnership for New Education was responsible for the institution of PDSs, PDSs were not initiated as a school-by-school quid pro quo contract between the university and schools. The important realization for urban schooling is that most PDSs are arrived at as a part of a larger initiative with funding sources that are not likely to be available to under-resourced urban school districts for the specific purpose of creating a PDS. Despite its appeal (recall the category one meaning of PDS as partnership), a PDS is not something that a school or a university can unilaterally establish. Moreover, those partnership arrangements pursued by individual schools and universities independent of funding sources and organized initiatives are likely to be among those regarded as "erzatz PDSs" because they do not meet the standards of a "true PDS" (Levine, 1995).

2. The PDS is an invention coming from a *history* of collaboration between universities and public schools, not the other way around. To a large extent, PDS is a coined term for what has already existed. Most of the popular appeal of the PDS idea inheres with the fact that people regard collaboration as a good idea, without realizing that collaboration is *not* synonymous with a PDS. Many who value collaboration may not even be aware of the particular configuration of purposes,

goals, and organizational structures of the PDS as articulated by the Holmes Group and others. The report (Judge et al., 1995) notes:

> Although there is of course a long tradition of collaboration between universities and public schools (exemplified in the lab schools and other more recent but ephemeral initiatives), the PDS as it has emerged in Michigan is essentially a creation of the reform movements of the later 1980s. (section 4)

PDS is popularly known because the notion of collaborative partnership is a good idea and has a history as a good idea.

3. The reviewers found that being a PDS did make a difference. However, the difference—"sustained efforts to change and improve the culture and effectiveness of whole school" (Judge et al., 1995, section 9)—is the one result that *does not require a PDS framework* to bring about. Apparently, the enthusiasm and heightened activity generated by their status as a PDS school influenced the schools' professional activity.

4. The efficacy evidence was underwhelming for the work in diverse urban contexts, underscoring a feature of the great school reforms observed by Sarason (1993) years ago—that professional activity can take place without commensurate results in student performance. The reviewers wrote: "The Review team was (before, during and after its visits) much preoccupied with this issue and in particular with the relative paucity of evidence on the extent to which specific and measurable improvements in student learning had in fact occurred" (Judge et al., 1995, section 10).

5. Even in this review document, where reviewers call for evidence, there was no specification of indicators that related to the quality of learning, leading them to suggest:

> For the purposes of evaluating PDS effects on students it would be necessary to complement such necessary information with other indicators, including various forms of standardized testing, portfolio assessments, attendance information, dropout rates, report card grades, and teacher evaluation. (Judge et al., 1995, section 11)

Those who understand the ways and needs of urban schools and communities would add to this list those forms of evidence drawn from the experiences of the students themselves, and from their parents, their families, and others who work with the children on a daily basis.

6. PDSs often are not financially independent agents, but rather are funded through larger scale initiatives. So, for example, even those fortunate to have PDS status may be at risk for discontinued funding and have to compete with other PDSs for resources, as was the case in Michigan:

> The MPNE made it clear that it would no longer be able to support the PDSs at their present level, and indeed began late in 1994 to define different priorities for its own work. The two Co-Directors of the PDS program at MSU explained the situation to the PDSs, which were invited to bid for future support. (Judge et al., 1995, section 7)

This is a useful insight for those considering an urban PDS. PDSs in urban districts are often at a resource disadvantage for the process of soliciting grants. To pursue a PDS or even participate as a grantee involves a commitment of resources that may otherwise be diverted from the immediate, day-to-day work of improving instruction for children. This is the best example of what one parent organizer calls the "great white school reform"—by which she meant the large-scale, bureaucratic initiatives emanating from central administration that rarely seek input or participation by the people affected, and, worse yet, make no difference in the lives of children (anonymous personal communication). This parent organizer included PDSs under that label, regarding them as way of reshuffling the organization of a school and expending resources, without accessing the local knowledge emanating from parent organizations and from people who actually work with the children on a daily basis.

One reason why it is rare to find PDSs with all of the characteristics of the universalized goals as put forward by NCREST (1993) is that there is no generic PDS start-up. Interestingly, MSU regarded PDSs not as a stand-alone initiative, but rather as a component in the total program of the MPNE. According to the MSU Report (Judge et al., 1995), what propelled the PDS idea to the forefront was the availability of public funding from the state department of education and from the legislature. The report states:

> The fortunes of the PDS and MPNE were entangled in a way which inevitably generated tensions. As dollars became more easily available for noble reforming causes, so the pace of development become correspondingly more hectic. It was difficult in such an atmosphere to argue the general case for the PDS without seeking to universalize the institution, and yet

many of those thoughtfully *dedicated to the core arguments for the new institutions feared that rapid expansion would inevitably damage their viability and credibility.* Doubts about a bold and rapid expansion of PDSs were easily confused with opposition to the PDS itself, or even to the leadership of the College as it was often perceived [emphasis added]. (section 6)

Problem Four—Inadequacy of PDS Theory

PDSs are not designed to address the underlying political questions that produce inequities in schooling. As a result of the disconnectedness of the PDS organizational structure from the wider community, theoretical frameworks for interrogating such questions in their pedagogical inquiry are inadequate. The theoretical frameworks needed are not strictly academic, but should include systematic inquiry about how the school functions as a community, a culture, and a public space within neighborhoods. There is much in the PDS literature that acknowledges the importance of situating professional development in the local, purposeful, problem-solving endeavors of individual school communities (Darling-Hammond, 1994; Lieberman, 1995; Little, 1993, 1994; Miller & O'Shea, 1994; Myers, 1996b; Vavrus, 1995). But reviews of the current PDS literature reveal scant attention to building communities of practice (cf. Valli et al., 1997; Teitel, 1996).

Rarely apparent in the PDS literature are the pedagogical practices or foundational theory underlying actual school practices. Rather, reference to the driving conceptual ideas are made on the bases of the popularized ideas—among them are constructivism, child-centered learning, cooperative learning, and multiple intelligences. Valli (1994) makes this observation:

> Too often, words like "school improvement" function as a gloss. They represent "superficially attractive appearances" which cover up or ignore fundamental questions such as "What is it we are trying to improve? How? Why? For whose benefit?" A term like school improvement can give license to any type of change or reform without any agreement on (sometimes without any discussion of) the direction, benefit, or purpose or change. (p. 1)

The preponderance of PDS efficacy research is characterized by descriptive studies that employ analyses that fail to account for the relationship between practices and the social-cultural context in which those practices are employed in teaching and learning. Lacking a framework that unifies three levels of analysis—classroom practice (micro), inter-professional reflective practice (meso), and organizational-institutional structure (macro)—leaves PDS research with little else to reference in their theory and practice other than catch words of the day (e.g., constructivism, child-centered learning). The unfortunate consequence is that these become buzz words in the popular culture of teachers and are used to roughly separate the "innovative, new, and good" from the "traditional, old, and bad."

The indexing of the foundational theory in PDS work by catch words is problematic for other reasons. First, research of this type does not further the PDS chartering goal of reflective pedagogical inquiry—understanding the relationships between practices and the building of a learning community. Second, interpretations of research of this type are problematic to the extent to which they uncritically assume that terms like "child-centered learning" or "constructivist teaching" mean the same thing to everyone. Third, as Valli (1994) points out, to say that change occurs in measures of "constructivist teaching" or "child-centered learning" simply begs the question as to whether these changes are of any value.

Neither universalizing nor operationalizing definitions for the collection of terms referring to "innovative practice" will help PDS research of this type because what interested readers need to know and understand is how "constructivist teaching" or "child-centered teaching" benefit learning achievement in the learning community. Part of the critical re-interpretation of the new knowledge base should therefore include semiotic analysis of such constructs in context (cf. Brown, Collins, & Duguid, 1989; Bruner, 1990; Harre & Gillet, 1994; Lave, 1992; Lemke, 1997). Hargreaves (1995) has begun this examination by looking at the extent to which the PDS framework has become a signifier—a symbol for the "good school" and the "good work" in teacher preparation (p. 30).

Summary

The organization of collaborative partnerships must be informed by what we know about the practices of effective urban education, particularly for children of color (e.g., Ladson-Billings, 1994; Shujaa, 1994; Foster, 1989, 1992; King, Hollings, & Hayman, 1997; King & Ladson-Billings, 1990). In the climate of current reform agendas that have, historically, threatened equity considerations (e.g., movement toward standardized testing) it is unclear whether equity issues can ever adequately be addressed within the PDS framework. The particular needs of culturally diverse children are rarely addressed in the PDS literature beyond the mention of general statistics pertaining to the race and socioeconomic status of students. According to Valli et al., (1997), contextual and cultural dimensions of education are rarely systematically examined in PDS work and are peripherally related to its goals and activities.

PDS work to date lacks the critical perspective on race, class, culture, and power that is necessary to build learning communities or communities of practice. Both Apple (1986) and Hargreaves (1995) warn of professional development as intensification where the replication of *what is* takes priority over visioning *what should be*. When applied as a model for structuring a collaboration, there is an inherent limitation to the inclusion of important participants owing to the bilateral arrangement between school and university professionals. Parents, youth workers, and other school-based personnel—and the pupils themselves—are locked out because of the "sanctity of the profession" occupied by teachers and university faculty.

Finally, there are serious constraints and inherent (perhaps insurmountable problems) with the PDS bilateral organizational framework in which only university personnel and school personnel have a "seat at the table." Consideration of parents and community stakeholders are therefore, by default, *ad hoc*. The ostensible goal of the PDS arrangement is to build a new organization in the school which includes a *system of professional development* as well as a *community of practice* designed to realize, for example, the seven NCREST (1993) vision statements. The practical result of most PDSs, according to the evidence of comprehensive reviews (e.g., Valli et al., 1997; Teitel, 1996) is neither a new organizational structure nor the simultaneous renewal of school and university contexts.

3
A NEW CONCEPTUAL FRAMEWORK FOR PDSs IN URBAN SETTINGS

> Having high expectations for students, cultural congruence of instruction, culturally inclusive curriculum, knowledgeable teachers, and appropriate instructional strategies all contribute to narrowing the achievement gap in urban schools. However, by themselves they are still not enough to overcome the effects of racism, language discrimination, and a history of discrimination against poor people of color. (Zeichner, 1996, p. 67)

The essential feature of successful school improvement in urban contexts as expressed by advocates of the PDS idea is that of linking the development of teachers to student work and learning achievement. As demonstrated in the last chapter, this connection is the missing piece of the PDS framework for successful school development in urban contexts. This PDS shortcoming manifests itself in the lack of connection between children's experience of curriculum and instruction on the one hand, and the policies, procedures, and organization of the PDS partnership on the other hand. The discontinuity between student outcomes and teacher development results from the inordinate and atheoretical PDS focus on "improving teaching" at the expense of attention to the social and cultural contexts of learning—analyses essential for developing responsive teaching practice in diverse urban communities.

In this chapter, I will develop a framework which extends the PDS model in ways that address the current shortcomings. One part of the challenge of developing a conceptual framework is addressing the issue of *tooling up of teachers* instead of the development of *communities of practice*. Another challenge lies in the insufficiency of the current theoretical frameworks—modernist educational theory in a postmodern world. A third challenge for developing new theory is the problem of how to interrogate the political and ideological dynamics in our national policies toward education—and the problem of uncritical engagement with these policies in the constitution of PDSs.

A new conceptual framework should integrate at least three levels of inquiry: (1) a micro level addressing development of the individual learners in classroom contexts; (2) a meso level addressing development of the relationships constituting the social, cultural, and professional fabric of the school community; and (3) a macro level addressing development of broader institutional, neighborhood, family, and support systems. Note the emphasis on *development* in each. I now turn to discussion of theory that does integrate these three theoretical-analytic tasks by developing the ideas of community of practice (after Lave, 1988, 1991, 1992), activity setting, and triadic restructuring (after Tharp & Gallimore, 1991).

Community of Practice—
Activity Settings for Teaching and Learning

In the PDS literature, there is continuous and frequent use of such terms as learning communities, learning collaboratives, and communities of learning to refer to the importance of connecting the instructional to the institutional in developing collaboratives. This is roughly the idea of activity setting. Therefore, for this discussion I will follow the usage of activity setting by Tharp and Gallimore (1991) and adopt the term. Briefly, the term denotes the unit of analysis to unpack the social, cultural, and interactional context for both teacher development and student achievement, in the same way it has been used to unpack contextual and discursive features of instructional settings.

The idea of activity setting is analogous to what cognitive psychologists have referred to as schemata (Rumelhart, 1980) and scripts (Schank & Abelson, 1977). According to Tharp and Gallimore's (1991) characterization, they are the recognizable "social furniture" of familiar settings in which people are engaged in meaningful cojoint activity:

> They are as homely and familiar as old shoes on the front porch. They are the social furniture of our family, community, and our home lives. They are the events and people of our work and relations to one another. They are the who, what, when, where and why, the small recurrent dramas of everyday life, played on the stages of home, school, community, and workplace.... (p. 72)

The activity setting, as a unit of analysis, focuses inquiry on the setting in which some cojoint purposeful activity is being carried out—

a familiar occasion or setting, perhaps routine, perhaps ritualized. The idea of the activity setting is essential to the tasks of school development. *Instructional activity settings* within classrooms include such things as independent learning centers, cooperative learning groups, reading groups, and whole class instruction. *Professional activity settings* include such things as staff meetings, team meetings, and conferences. Teacher capacity to develop activity settings is the linchpin of developing learning communities of effective practice.

Before leaving this description of the micro level of inquiry and pedagogical theory reformulations of the PDS idea for work in urban schools, I will make two points regarding the relevance of the activity setting (for further information, see Murrell, n.d.). The first point is that to organize a community of practice, participants in a partnership need to be able to analyze and assess the activity settings of their professional work. This means analyzing the social-interactional dynamics and the purposes of collaborative activity, as well as the meaning participants attach to that activity, in order to determine appropriate policies, tasks, and strategies.

The second point is that the central activity setting of the professional development school—the clinical triad—must be extended and elaborated in order to respond to broader social, political, and cultural concerns. Recall that the clinical triad is the setting of the clinical three-way interview or conference between the college supervisor, the cooperating teacher at the site, and the beginning teacher or intern. In current practice in PDSs, this activity setting is the primary means by which the novice teacher receives systematic vocal feedback from both the college supervisor and practitioner. Ideally, the setting should provide the integration of theory and practice through the participation of the college supervisor and cooperating teacher. But, too often, it does not.

When complex ideological issues arise requiring deep cultural interpretation, they often are not addressed in the context in which they most need to be. Such issues may in fact polarize the university and school faculty, leaving the candidate with the continued schism of "ivory tower" versus "real world" versions of difficult issues. The three-way conference is an activity setting in which relationships must be negotiated before it can function as a facilitative and instructional setting for the beginning teacher. The learning experience of the candidate may be diminished to the extent that the cooperating teacher and college supervisor disagree on policies, pedagogy, or practice. But, the problem may be more even more complex.

Complex issues do not exist in a vacuum. Successful negotiation of an issue among participants in a clinical triad may simply mean that an important issue for the school is smoothed over. The goal of successful collaboration is to dramatically amplify the possibilities of the three-way conference as an activity setting that provides the authentic context for struggling though a resolution to difficult issues. The activity setting on this account has to be worked on, so that rather than a temporary resolution, the larger issue is brought to the entire school community of the collaborative. Resolutions of difficult issues cannot and should not be accomplished in a single setting, nor in any number of discussions in university seminars or school conferences. Resolutions need to be instantiated in the practices and policies of the school influencing the lives of real children.

The task of developing a professional development system is, on this account, to create an activity setting among teachers for the purposes of improved instruction. The goal is to build a new community of practice. One of the important aspects of doing this is to enrich the tasks of professional development by creating activity settings other than the three-way conference to support teachers' practice. The goal is to increase the number of non-formal sources of assistance. Tharp and Gallimore (1991) note:

> Effective teaching does not require authority. The assistance of performance can sometimes be provided more effectively in its absence. Even authorities can assist performance only through the exercise of modeling, contingency managing, feeding back, questioning, and cognitive structuring. 'Rather than teaching being dependent on authority, it is more nearly the opposite; indeed, teaching is the process on which authority depends to achieve its aims.' (p. 85)

The orchestration or creation of activity settings, therefore, is the single most essential capacity of a PDS educator. The task of professional development schools is to build communities of practice and activity settings, not simply to "tool up" the teachers, but primarily to develop activity settings in which everyone in the collaborative learns to improve practice. There is a need for the development of knowledge of individuals and of systems as they interact throughout a community of practice and enacted in an activity setting.

Community of Practice—
Activity Settings for School Development

The second aspect of a unified educational theory applied to the development of PDSs is the notion of the triadic analysis. This aspect corresponds to the meso level of inquiry. This idea is embodied in the formal statement of the Holmes Group (1990) regarding the need for a close connection of professional development with the learning of achievement of children. It is an extension of the notion of assisted performance from classroom instructional practice to the venue of professional activities. Triadic analysis is a simple, yet important, idea—that any assessment, evaluation, support, assistance, or scaffolding of teaching be done in connection with the resulting experiences and learning achievements of the students.

It is no secret that there are insufficient opportunities, resources, and personnel to accomplish the type of professional development activities popularly envisioned in the PDS advocacy literature. Moreover, this insufficiency makes it difficult for administrators to interact with teachers in a facilitative way, or, in turn, for superintendents to interact with principals in a facilitative way. The point is that activity settings, as described previously, must be created at all levels. This is the task of the professional development school—creating strategically designed activity settings that promote assistance at all levels of the school organization but still are linked to the learning achievements of the students in the school.

One of the positive things about the PDS movement is that it encourages approaches to professional development as a co-joint productive activity, where the production is new professional knowledge and instructional innovation that makes a difference in the quality of schooling. The essential step is the involvement of university people and school people in the co-joint productive activity, coming together on the goal all can agree upon, improving the instructional quality and, consequently, elevating the learning achievement of all students in the school.

Most schools, including professional development schools, operate in a bureaucratic system characterized by a linear chain of command. In this sort of design, individual A (e.g., a superintendent) directs and evaluates individual B (e.g., a principal) who in turn directs and evaluates individual C (e.g., a classroom teacher). What the triadic analysis suggests is a different sort of organization of practice in which the functions of the setting are not primarily those of directing and evaluating, but rather providing assistance in creating a new culture of practice. This type of organization has certainly been identified often enough in the PDS literature as a desirable goal. However, what appears to be lacking is a systematic account or conceptual framework of how this is to come about.

A New Conceptual Framework

The basic formulation of a new conceptual framework for PDS work is threefold: (1) The function of direction, regulation, and evaluation are altered to that of assisting performance; (2) the means of assistance are to be mutual and reciprocal (bilateral) rather than hierarchical (unilateral); and (3) the lines of communication are expanded from a linear, sequential, top-down structure to an organization with multiple linkages. An example of this last point, is an organization in which individual A (e.g., a superintendent) assists individual B directly, as well as others (e.g., other principals) who can assist individual B; and individual B (e.g., a principal) assists individual C (e.g., a classroom teacher) directly and by creating conditions for others (e.g., other teachers) to assist C.

The function of the principal in an administrative role in this formulation shifts from the regulation and directing of individuals working under him or her, to creating the conditions under which the tasks of teaching and improving teaching are supported. The infrastructure provided by the idea of the activity setting and the analytical framework provided by the triadic analysis is described by Tharp and Gallimore (1991):

> Each position in the organization is restricted in its range of contacts. Most contact is with the next individual in the chain of supervision. In general then we can suggest that good work in each position consists in assisting the next position to assist the third and so forth down the chain for the ultimate benefit for the student. The good work of the superintendent lies in assisting the principal to assist the grade level chairs; their work consists of assisting in developing the children by assisting them through their zone of proximal development. (p. 84)

This approach of triadic analysis is dramatically different from supervision extant in most school bureaucracies whether or not they are PDSs. The presence of PDS partners does not change the bureaucratic structure of schools, according to Valli in her review of both the advocacy and research literature (Valli, 1994). There undoubtedly is a greater involvement of PDS teachers in school decision making. But, as the present analysis points out, there is a difference between tinkering with the activity setting (in this case by altering the participation structure for teachers) and substantially redesigning how the community of practice operates—which in most cases is still hierarchical, directive, and evaluative in a linear top-down fashion in contrast to the lateral, assisting, and multi-connected set of relationships suggested here.

Effective PDS development work requires a restructuring of the lines of responsibility and assistance. The triadic model and the conceptual framework of the activity setting are the most likely and theoretically developed means by which PDSs may begin the critical work of examining the social and cultural contexts of teaching and learning—to "reinvent" the school learning community.

The work of PDSs is the development of a true community of practice through triadic analysis and the transformation of the activity settings devoted to school improvement. The task of PDSs on this account is to enrich the working relationships in new activity settings that afford authentic and meaningful participation for parents and community stakeholders in the work that matters. The beginnings of unpacking the social-cultural context of teaching in relation to the organizational structure depends on the principles of triadic analysis and the notion of the activity setting that come from the conceptual framework discussed above, referred to as assisted performance (a synthesis of traditions from neo-Vygotskyan, Deweyan, situated cognition, and cognitive-learning theory). The principles of the triadic analysis and activity settings from Tharp and Gallimore (1991) are:

- Whether or not the supervisor is more competent than the supervisees for the task at hand, the ideal is for the supervisor to participate at all times in at least one activity setting with the supervisees.

- The authority of the supervisor should be exercised primarily to reorganize activity settings and to make resources of time, place, persons, and tools available to them. Within the activity setting, the authority of the supervisor should be shared with members of the setting, whose influences should be proportionate and specific to their competencies. The authority of the supervisor should be asserted within the activity setting only insofar as necessary to see the continuation of the setting. Authority should not override the emerging intersubjectivity and freedom in problem-solving of the activity's members.

- Each activity setting should have a product as its goal, a product that will be motivating for the participants, whether or not the ultimate goal of the supervisor is shared by the supervisees.

■ Each activity setting should have as its focus the ability of the supervisor to assist the supervisee; that is, A and B should focus on B's assisting of C. Obviously, the pupils have no supervisees; however, even pupils can be assisted to assist one another in settings of cooperative learning, *and students should be assisted to assist themselves.*

■ Activity settings should be either "permanent" or "temporary" as dictated by the goal and product.

■ Every member of the school community should be engaged in the joint productive activity of activity settings whose purpose is an ever-increasing competence to assist performance.

■ The task of every supervisor, from the board of education to the classroom teacher, is to design activity settings. This principle will create products, assist performance, foster intersubjectivities, promote the cognitive growth of each individual, refocus accountabilities, and turn schools into a culture of learning. (p. 92)

Community of Practice—The Macro Level of Inquiry

The most significant portions of the PDS movement are not so much what happens in professional development schools, which tend to recapitulate and fortify current practice, but in networks and larger school systems of PDSs which are able to take on the tasks of critique, reinvention of practice, and support of innovation. The goals of inquiry and reflective practice are not likely to be realized in any meaningful way at the level of individual PDS for the reasons elaborated by Murrell and Borunda (1997)—namely the "tyranny of the mundane." They will be realized from a community of practice that involves networks of participants from different PDSs serving similar community needs and interests. For urban education to make a point of respecting the wisdom of community people is not simply a political stance, it also embodies an important component of a powerful theory.

What would an urban-focused, equity-minded, diversity-responsive, and inquiry-based professional development school partnership look like? The nine features that follow are those that urban educators would expect to find if the critical professional knowledge teachers need for effective teaching and learning in diverse settings were applied (cf. Cochran-Smith, 1997; Grant, 1997; Hilliard, 1997; Irvine, 1996, 1997; Murrell, 1997). These features derive from a critical look at the social, cultural, historical, and political contexts of the schools we work in, and with, and for, armed with a critical perspective dedicated to learning from the shortcomings of models already in existence, especially our own (cf. Bowers & Flinders, 1990; Bruner, 1996).

A *"Quality of Education" Perspective*—Conceiving of "equity" in terms of practices that lead to quality education, as opposed to a conception of equity in terms of parity of resources. Critical interrogation of the conception of "educational equity" has been conspicuously absent in both the advocacy and research literature on PDSs. An urban-focused approach to professional development shifts from an "equality of schooling" or everyone-gets-the-same perspective, to a "quality of teaching and learning" perspective. On this account, we would no longer look at equity merely in terms of "racial balance" or equivalent numbers of books and computers, but primarily in terms of effect—whether children's experiences of the curriculum and scholastic achievement are actually improved.

A *"Collaborative, Multilateral Partnership" Perspective*—Partnership formation that is not only open to community constituencies—parents and parent organizations, community agencies who work with the same children, and other stakeholders—but also is open to co-joint collaboration with other institutions of higher education. On this account, alternatives that differ from the bilateral school-university partnership of the PDS model are pursued if they maximize the development of the school. Thus, the bilateral structure of the PDS model does not dictate the tasks (inservice and preservice development) and the collaboration is fully responsive to the needs, interests, and ongoing agendas of the school community.

A *"Positionality" Perspective*—The recognition that a teacher's work is not simply a matter of acquiring the appropriate skills, techniques, and expertise but ought also to include being politically reflective and ideologically interpretive. As Cochran-Smith (1997) argues, the development for effective work in urban sites "is about interpretation, ideologies, and practices" and the ways that these are interdependent with, and informed by, each other (p. 30). She rightly argues that teachers' knowledge from this perspective is not simply about skills and techniques, or what people frequently refer to as "best practice."

A *Community Development Agenda*—A focus on teacher preparation predicated on how to operate within the context of a community development agenda. Regardless of how well prepared teachers are, or how excellent the curriculum, children still cannot learn when they come to school hungry, angry, afraid, disaffected, unwell, or conflicted.

The total contexts in which children grow, learn, and develop are necessary considerations in promoting their academic achievement and personal development. This idea is best exemplified in the Comer (1997) model.

A *"Scholar-Teacher" Perspective*—A focus on "visioning" and developing a new kind of teacher for effectively meeting the challenges of successful work in urban schools and communities in the 21st century. This would require teacher preparation focused on a new and different kind of teacher who recognizes, understands, and effectively negotiates complexities of urban communities that impact children's learning and development.

A *"Relationships Over Bureaucracies" Perspective*—A patently anti-bureaucratic mode of interaction among partners that permits flexibility of collaboration that involves all stakeholders in the enterprise of educating and developing children. This flexible collaboration is required in order to invite the participation of parents, community members, and all stakeholders necessary for effective problem definition and resolution.

The most important feature we would expect to find in an urban-focused, equity-minded, diversity responsive, and inquiry-based PDS is attention to building democratic organizations in light of the social, cultural, and political realities of urban schools. Critical pedagogy is a perspective that encourages critical reflection about how we, as university people, enter into partnership with school communities. Critical pedagogy is a perspective that acknowledges that we do not fully know what to do and think until we couple our actions and thoughts with a process of joint public discourse and community building.

Consequently, our research, our theory, and our program development must be closely linked to the everyday practical activities of school and community development. This means the elimination of "helperism" in our relationship to our partners in urban communities, and working with them on *their* enterprises of change. From this perspective, the broader purpose of higher education in the life of urban communities ought to be as a participant in transforming these communities, as the means of moving society toward becoming a truly just, multicultural democracy. Therefore, the primary work of an urban-focused, equity-minded partnership is building community on a multiplicity of levels—both inter- and intra-institutional.

An *"Expanded Roles" Perspective*—As stated earlier, a public, community-centered, and child-focused approach to building partnerships is essential to the project of developing an urban-focused, equity-minded, diversity-responsive, and inquiry-based professional relationship. Otherwise, perspectives that need to be surfaced, confronted, and negotiated will remain unvoiced. But within this partnership-building, there are opportunities for individuals to assume roles of leadership, training, support, and policymaking that are broader than the ascribed roles of parent, teacher, or administrator.

A *"Community as Network of Relationships" Perspective*—The eighth point of the transition concerns what really cements the partnership between school personnel and non-school personnel—building community through our actual physical presence in the schools. The participants in partner schools are adamant and clear about this being the essential ingredient for cementing the partnership—that university and other non-school personnel spend time in the schools and in settings with children—the notion of "being there" (Murrell, 1991, p. 223). The measure of our success as agents for change is not the *expertise* we bring as university people, but rather our *capacity to learn in the company of others.* This vision engenders an active disbelief in deficits-based professional practice that targets "clients" as needy, pathological, and incompetent. This vision calls us to foster relational practices in our personal and professional interactions and in our invitations to those with whom we work.

A *"Joint Responsibility and Accountability" Perspective*—University *responsibility*—university and college partners sharing the responsibility for the gains in academic achievement and personal development of children in those communities, and *accountability* for lack of progress.

These nine features are developed into recommendations for reformulating an equity agenda in the context of this new professional development paradigm in Table 1 below.

Table 1. Summary of Contrasts between Traditional PDS Models and a New Concept of the Professional Development Community-Collaborative (PDCC)

Professional Development School Model	Model of an Equity Minded, Urban-Focused, and Culturally Responsive Partnership
1. Equity of Schooling Educational equity viewed in terms of *comparison* of the "haves" and the "have nots."	1. Quality of Teaching & Learning Educational equity viewed in terms of determining first what constitutes *quality education*, and then determining where it must be developed.
2. Standard Bilateral Structure The institutional relationship is *exclusively bilateral*—a college or university partners with a school or school district.	2. Flexible Multilateral Structure The institutional relationship not exclusive to a single university or to a single school in partnership, but a *multilateral*, multi-partnered collaborative including a diversity of institutional stakeholders (e.g., the schools in a "cluster" along with all the youth-oriented and community-based organizations in those neighborhoods).
3. Development of Teachers Focus is on the *professional development of teachers* and improving teaching as the foundation of restructuring of public education.	3. Development of Teachers' Positionality as Agents in Communities Focus is on the *development of teachers, parents, schools, neighborhoods and, most importantly, children* as the foundation of restructuring and renewing public education.
4. Teacher Focused Agenda The dynamic of the partnership is a quid pro quo type of *mutuality in the exchange of services and resources*—teaching and clinical placements for the university, resources and training for the school.	4. Community Development Agenda The dynamic of the partnership is *community development*—the mobilization of available resources within the "cluster" and eliciting community capacity for solving problems and managing dilemmas.

Table 1 *continued.*

Professional Development School Model	Model of an Equity Minded, Urban-Focused, and Culturally Responsive Partnership
5. **Teacher as Expert Pedagogue** Teacher preparation more in the tradition of the "lab school" model that is top-down in design with little community or school-based input.	5. **Teacher as Teacher-Scholar** *Teacher preparation focused on a new and different kind* of teacher whose practice is based on critical inquiry and who recognizes, understands, and effectively negotiates complexities of urban communities that impact children's learning and development.
6. **Bureaucratic Orientation** Contractual arrangements and/or *formal agreements* are the cement of the working relationship.	6. **Community-Building Orientation** Community organization and *community building* are the cement of working relationships.
7. **Delimited Unitary Roles** Professionally *circumscribed roles* for participants—parents participating as parents, practitioners as practitioners, professors as professors.	7. **Diversifying Multiple Roles** *Multiple roles* for participants—e.g., parents as trainers of teachers, parents as planners, and policy makers.
8. **Community as Geographic Area** *Tendency to define "community" according to geographic area*—the actual boundaries of an area of the city.	8. **Community as Network of Relationships Bound by Common Interest and Commitment** Tendency to *define "community" in terms of relationship bonds* among those individuals having the same goals, purposes, and commitments with respect to children and families in a geographic area.
9. **School Accountability** Program evaluation focus is based on *congruence to the model, not performance*—increasingly based on how well the partnership conforms to the standards of the PDS model.	9. **Joint Accountability for Student Success** Program evaluation of the success of the collaborative partnership with respect to *measurable and demonstrable improvements in children's academic achievement, personal development, and well-being.*

CONCLUSIONS

I conclude this monograph in a different tone and a different voice, speaking directly to those of you who may be embarking on a PDS enterprise. I want to speak particularly to my colleagues in teacher preparation and higher education.

At this point you may be thinking: "This was all well and good, but where are the models?" If this question is uppermost in the reader's mind, I have not succeeded in pressing home my main thesis. The appeal of the PDS model distorts the work of developing children and schools in urban communities. I did not in any way want to privilege the idea of models over a new kind of "knowing how" based on the integration of the cultural heritage of achievement in communities of color.

Do not misunderstand me; I am not anti-model. As a cognitive psychologist, trained during the heyday of information processing models, schema theory, and mental modeling, I understand the value of a good model. But, that is not what is at issue here. What is at issue is how we make use of what we know, in ways that do not replicate what we are trying to remedy. This issue is about institutional boundedness and the extent to which our professional penchant for models is part of the invisible culture of academy that blinds us to what we really need to see. It is not that models don't matter. What matters is the use we make of our representations.

The "know how" to which I refer is based upon a deep understanding of *what it means to make community.* Obviously, people make communities—and people living in community have to work at maintaining it. But, I refer here to community building as thoughtful, intentional, and collaborative professional action. In this age of social crisis and distorted national priorities, it is a fresh look at practices of community building that will make change possible. Taking this fresh look, with the humility of good anthropology, is antithetical to the method we educationalists usually take. We see something working, and right away it becomes the model that we should "replicate" elsewhere. Just click on the icon, cut, and paste. The problem is that icon, or symbol, is not the thing.

I am convinced that more harm than good comes from this models orientation as exemplified by the PDS movement; particularly when I see how our colleagues think about what applying a model means. For example, recently I heard some colleagues talking about the X-model of their PDS, where "X" is the name of an anonymous university. I was intrigued by the ascription of the label "model" and began to interview this group of educators from the PDS as to what features earned the partnership the status as a "model." It turned out that the distinguishing feature was that the student teaching seminar was held at the site of the PDS instead of at the university. Despite the fact that virtually every other institution in the area had done the same thing in their teacher education programs at some time or another, in the minds of this group of people this single feature characterized the X-model.

The recognition of human systems as a model tends to reduce it to a symbol and obscure the richness and detail of a community. The way that the program was reduced to this particular feature, and the way that all the unique and possibly innovative features of the program became obscured, convinced me that any talk of "models" in our work is problematic and misguided. Approaches to professional collaboration that are institutionally bounded by the invisible cultures of school bureaucracies are made worse if we look for the generalizable instead of recognizing the richness of relationships.

Much of what needs to happen in building a school community involves developing human activity by thinking about oneself in relation to others. This involves asking such questions as "What kind of society do I want to live in? And, "What kind of society do I want my children, and my children's children to grow up in?" It is in asking these questions that you begin to connect the simple, ordinary, everyday choices you make to the larger workings of our democracy. In reality, this is the most important reflection that anyone does as one thinks about his or her relationship with others and the institutions of global community. This is the reflection that should be an explicit part of community building in collaborative partnerships.

Contemplating where one's self ends and the rest of humanity begins is the basis of our understanding of ourselves, our community, and our institutions. Everyone, at some point, necessarily thinks about self in relation to the world. Moreover, this process of rethinking, perhaps remaking, ourselves in relationship to others is an ongoing process. The challenge for us as professionals contemplating collaborative partnerships in urban settings is not to make models, but to make connections to the lives of those we hope to influence for the better.

What this means in practice is an approach exemplified by James Comer (1997), the one model I will endorse because it is a design for the development of a school community that begins with the children. It is time to begin organizing the contexts of our practice in ways that develop the "know how" to support those ends.

REFERENCES

Abdal-Haqq, I. (1996). Locating resources on professional development schools. ERIC Digest 95-3, Washington, DC: ERIC Clearinghouse on Teaching and Teacher Education.

Abdal-Haqq, I. (1997). Resources on professional development schools: An annotated bibliography and resource guide. Washington, D.C.: American Association of Colleges for Teacher Education and ERIC Clearinghouse on Teaching and Teacher Education.

Abdal-Haqq, I. (1998). Professional development schools: Weighing the evidence. Thousand Oaks, CA: Corwin Press.

Apple, M. (1986). Teachers and texts: A political economy of class and gender relations in education. New York: Routledge.

Bordieu, P., & Passeron, C. (1977). Reproduction in education, society, and culture. Beverly Hills, CA: Sage Publications.

Bowers, C. A., & Flinders, D. J. (1990). Responsive teaching: An ecological approach to classroom patterns of language, culture and thought. New York: Teachers College Press.

Bowles, S., & Gintes, H. (1976). Schooling in capitalist America. New York: Basic Books.

Brown, J. S., Collins, A., and Duguid, P. (1989). Situated cognition and the culture of learning. Educational Researcher, 18(1), 32-42.

Brown, M. (1947). Stone soup. New York: Charles Scribner's Sons.

Bruner, J. (1990). Acts of meaning. Cambridge, MA: Harvard University Press.

Bruner, J. (1996). The culture of education. Cambridge, MA: Harvard University Press.

The Carnegie Forum on Education and the Economy. (1986). A Nation Prepared: Teachers for the 21st century. Washington, DC: Carnegie Forum on Education and the Economy.

Cochran-Smith, M. (1997). Knowledge, skills, and experiences for teaching culturally diverse learners: A perspective for practicing teachers. In J.J. Irvine (Ed.), Critical knowledge for diverse teachers and learners (pp. 27-88). Washington, DC: American Association of Colleges for Teacher Education.

Comer, J. P. (1997). Waiting for a miracle: Why schools can't solve our problems and why we can. New York: Penguin Putnam Inc.

Darling-Hammond, L. (1992, July). Standards of practice for learner-centered schools. New York: National Center for Restructuring Education, Schools, and Teaching, Teachers College, Columbia University.

Darling-Hammond, L. (Ed.). (1994). Professional development schools: Schools for developing a profession. New York: Teachers College Press.

Darling-Hammond, L., Lieberman, A., McLauglin, M., & Miller, L. (1992). Professional development and reconstructuring. New York: National Center for Restructuring Education, Schools, and Teaching, Teachers College, Columbia University.

Delpit, L. D. (1988). The silenced dialog: Power and pedagogy in educating other people's children. *Harvard Educational Review, 58*(3), 280-298.

Foster, M. (1989). It's cooking now: A performance analysis of the speech events of a Black teacher in an urban community college. Language and Society, *18*(1), 1-29.

Foster, M. (1992). Urban African American teachers' views of organizational change: Speculations on the experiences of exemplary teachers. Paper prepared for the Center on Organization and Restructuring of Schools; The Wisconsin Center for Education Research, School of Education, University of Wisconsin-Madison. OERI Grant No R117Q00005-92.

Freire, P. (1970/1993). Pedagogy of the oppressed. New York: Continuum Publishing Company.

Giroux, H. A. (1991). Border crossings: Cultural workers and the politics of education. New York: Routledge.

2). Educational leadership and the crisis of demo-
ent. Educational Researcher, 21(4), 4-11.

J. (1991). Teachers for our nation's schools. San Francisco:
bass.

dlad, J. (1988). School-university partnerships for educational re-
wal: Rationale and concepts. In K. Sirotnik & J. Goodlad (Eds.),
chool-university partnerships in action: Concepts, cases and concerns
(pp. 3-31). New York: Teachers College Press.

Goodlad, J. (1994). Education renewal: Better teachers, better schools.
San Francisco: Jossey-Bass.

Grant, C. (1997). Critical knowledge, skills, and experiences for the
instruction of culturally diverse students: A perspective for the preparation of preservice teachers. In J.J. Irvine (Ed.), Critical knowledge for
diverse teachers and learners (pp. 1-26). Washington, DC: American
Association of Colleges for Teacher Education.

Hargreaves, A. (1994). Changing teachers, changing times: Teachers' work
and culture in the postmodern age. New York: Teachers College Press.

Hargreaves, A. (1995). Toward a social geography of teacher education. In N. K. Shimahara & I. Z. Holowinsky (Eds.), Teacher education
in industrialized nations: Issues in changing social contexts. (pp. 30-
40), New York: Garland Publishing.

Hargreaves, A., & Jacka, N. (1995). Induction or seduction? Postmodern
patterns of preparing teachers to teach. Peabody Journal of Education,
70(3), 41-63.

Harre, R. & Gillet, G. (1994). The Discursive Mind. Thousand Oaks,
CA: Sage Publications.

Hilliard, A. (1997). Teacher education from an African American perspective. In J.J. Irvine (Ed.), Critical knowledge for diverse teachers
and learners (pp. 125-148). Washington, DC: American Association of
Colleges for Teacher Education.

Holmes Group. (1986a). Tomorrow's schools of education. East Lansing, MI: Author.

Holmes Group. (1986b). Tomorrow's teachers. East Lansing, MI: Author.

Holmes Group. (1990). Tomorrow's schools. East Lan

Irvine, J. J. (1997). Creating and sustaining diverse comm
challenge of the Holmes Group. An Evaluation of the Holm
Agenda.

Irvine, J. J. (1997) Location, location, location: A synthesis perspec
on the knowledge base for urban teacher education. In J.J. Irvine (Ed
Critical knowledge for diverse teachers and learners (pp. 217-222). Wash
ington, DC: American Association of Colleges for Teacher Education.

Judge, H., Carriedo, R., & Johnson, S. M. (1995). Professional development schools and MSU. The report of the 1995 review. East Lansing,
MI: Michigan State University.

King, J. E., Hollings, E. R., & Hayman, W. C. (1997). Preparing teachers for cultural diversity. New York: Teachers College Press.

King, J. E., & Ladson-Billings, G. (1990). The teacher education challenge in elite university settings: Developing a critical perspective for
teaching in a democratic society. European Journal of Intercultural
Studies, 1(2), 15-25.

Labaree, D. F., & Pallas, A. M. (1996). Dire straits: The narrow vision
of the Holmes Group. Educational Researcher, 25(4), 25-28.

Ladson-Billings, G. (1994). The dreamkeepers: Successful teachers of
African American children. San Francisco: Jossey-Bass.

Lave, J. (1988). Cognition and practice. Cambridge, UK; Cambridge
University Press.

Lave, J. (1991). Situated learning in communities of practice. In L. B.
Resnick, J. M. Levine, & S. D. Teasley (Eds.). Perspectives on socially
shared cognition (p. 63-82). Washington, DC: American Psychological
Association.

Lave, J. (1992, April). Learning as participation in communities of practice. Paper presented at annual meeting of the American Educational
Research Association, San Francisco.

Lave, J. (1997). The culture of acquisition and the practice of understanding. In D. Kirshner & J. A. Whitson (Eds.), Situated cognition:

Social, semiotic, and psychological perspectives (pp. 17-36). Mahwah, NJ: Lawrence Erlbaum Associates.

Lawson, H. A. (1996). Expanding the Goodlad agenda: Interprofessional education and community collaboraton in service of vulnerable children, youth, and families. Holistic Education Review, 9(1), 20-34.

Lemke, J. L. (1997). Situated cognition: Social, semiotic, and psychological perspectives (pp. 37- 55). In D. Kirshner & J. A. Whitson (Eds.), Mahwah, NJ: Lawrence Erlbaum Associates.

Levine, M. (1995, Feb. 1). 21st century professional education: How education could learn from medicine, business, and engineering. (Commentary) Education Week, pp. 33-36.

Lieberman, A. (1995). Practices that Support Teacher Development: Transforming Conceptions of Professional Learning. Phi Delta Kappan, 76(8), 591-596.

Lieberman, A., & Miller, L. (1990). Teacher development in professional practice schools. Teachers College Record, 92(1), 105-112.

Little, J. W. (1994). Teachers' professional development in a climate of educational reform. In R. H. Anson (Ed.), Systematic reform: Perspectives on personalizing education (pp. 105-135). Washington, DC: U. S. Department of Education, Office of Educational Research and Improvement.

Little, J. W. (1993). Teachers' professional development in a climate of educational reform. Educational Evaluation and Policy Analysis, 15(2), 129-151.

Meier, T. R. (1982). Open admissions in black and white colleges: A comparative review. Unpublished manuscript.

Melnick, S. L., & Zeichner, K. M. (1997). Enhancing the capacity of teacher education institutions to address diversity issues. In J. E. King, E. R. Hollins, & W. C. Hayman (Eds.), Preparing teachers for cultural diversity (pp. 23- 39). New York: Teachers College Press.

Miller, L., & O'Shea, C. (1994). Partnership: Getting broader, getting deeper. NCREST reprint series. New York: National Center for Restructuring Education, Schools, and Teaching. Teachers College, Columbia University.

Murrell, P. C., Jr., (1991). Cultural politics in teacher education: What's missing in the preparation of African-American teachers? In M. Foster (Ed.) Readings on Equal Education, Vol. 11, (pp. 205–225).

Murrell, P. C., Jr., (1994). In search of responsive teaching for African American males: An investigation of students' experience of middle school mathematics curriculum. The Journal of Negro Education, 63(4), 556-569.

Murrell, P. C., Jr., (1997). Digging again the family wells: A Freirian literacy framework as emancipatory pedagogy for African American children. In P. Freire, J. Fraser, D. Macedo, T. McKinnon, & W. Stokes (Eds.), Mentoring the mentor: A critical dialog with Paulo Freire. Albany, NY: SUNY Press.

Murrell, P. C., Jr., (n.d.). Culture, cognition and communities of practice: Developing the exemplary urban school for African American children.

Murrell, P. C., Jr., & Borunda, M. (1997). The cultural and community politics of educational equity: Towards a new framework of professional development schools. Unpublished manuscript. National Center for Restructuring Education, Schools, and Teaching, Teachers College, Columbia University.

Murrell, P. C., Jr., & Diez, M. E. (1997). A model program for educating teachers for diversity. In J. E. King, E. R. Hollins, & W. C. Hayman (Eds.), Preparing teachers for cultural diversity (pp. 113-128). New York: Teachers College Press.

Myers, C. B. (1996a, April). Beyond the PDS: Schools as professional learning communities. A proposal based on an analysis of PDS efforts of the 1990s. Paper presented at the Annual Meeting of the American Educational Research Association, New York.

Myers, C. B. (1996b, April). University-school collaborations: A need to reconceptualize schools as professional learning communities instead of partnerships. Paper presented at the Annual Meeting of the American Educational Research Association, New York.

National Center for Restructuring Education, Schools, and Teaching [NCREST]. (1993). Vision statement of the Professional Development Schools Network. PDS: Professional Development Schools, 1(1), 3-4.

National Commission on Teaching & America's Future. (1996). What matters most: Teaching for America's future. Report of the National Commission on Teaching & America's Future. Carnegie Corporation of New York and Rockefeller Foundation. New York: Author.

Ponessa, (1997, March). Professional-Development Schools Stir Debate. Education Week, 16(25), 5.

Rumelhart, D. (1980). Schemata: The building blocks of cognition. In R. J. Spiro, B. C. Bruce, & W. F. Brewer (Eds.), Theoretical issues in reading and comprehension (pp. 33-58). Mahwah, NJ: Lawrence Erlbaum Associates.

Sarason, S. (1993). The case for change: Rethinking the preparation of teacher educators. San Francisco: Jossey-Bass.

Schack, G., & Overturf, B. J. (1994, April). Professonal development teams: Stepping stone (or next best thing) to professional development schools. Paper presented at the Annual Meeting of the American Educational Research Association, New Orleans.

Schank, R. C., & Abelson, R. (1977). Scripts, plans, goals and understanding. Mahwah, NJ: Lawrence Erlbaum Associates.

Shujaa, M. J. (1994). Education and schooling: Can you have one without the other? In M. J. Shujaa (Ed.) Too much schooling, too little education: A paradox in black life in white societies. Trenton, NJ: African World Press, Inc.

Teitel, L. (1996). Professional development schools: A literature review. Unpublished manuscript. Available from the Professional Development School Standards Project, National Council for Accreditation of Teacher Education (NCATE), Washington, D.C.

Teitel, L. (1997). Professional development schools and the transformation of teacher leadership. Teacher Education Quarterly, 24(1), 9-22.

Tharp, R. G., & Gallimore, R. (1991). Rousing minds to life: Teaching, learning and schooling in social context. Cambridge, England: Cambridge University Press.

Valli, L. (1994, April). Professional development schools: An opportunity to reconceptualize schools and teacher education as empowering learning communities. Paper presented at the Annual Meeting of the International Seminar on Teacher Education (ISTE), Maastricht, The Netherlands.

Valli, L., Cooper, D., & Frankes, L. (1997). Professional development schools and equity: A critical analysis of rhetoric and research. In M. W. Apple (Ed.), Review of research in education, 22 (pp. 251-304). Washington, DC: American Educational Research Association.

Vavrus, M. (1995, Spring-Summer). Tomorrow's Schools of Education: The Holmes Group. Educational Studies, 26(1/2), 135-139.

Wagner, T. (1995). What's school really for, anyway? And who should decide? Phi Delta Kappan, 76(5), 393-398.

Wagner, T. (1997). The new village commons—Improving schools together. Educational Leadership, 54(5), 25-28.

Walkerdine, V. (1997). Redefining the subject in situated cognition theory. In D. Kirshner & J. A. Whitson (Eds.), Situated cognition: Social, semiotic, and psychological perspectives (pp. 57-82). Mahwah, NJ: Lawrence Erlbaum Associates.

Williams, B. (Ed.). (1996). Closing the achievement gap: A vision for changing beliefs and practices. Alexandria, VA: Association for Supervision and Curriculum Development.

Woodson, C. G. (1933/1990). The miseducation of the negro. Washington, DC: Africa World Press.

Zeichner, K. M. (1996). Educating teachers to close the achievement gap: Issues of pedagogy, knowledge and teacher preparation. In B. Williams, (Ed.), Closing the achievement gap: A vision for changing beliefs and practices (pp. 56-76). Alexandria, VA: Association for Supervision and Curriculum Development.